YOU MATTER

Paul Wade

Loop Theory Volume 1

Copyright © 2025 Paul Wade

All rights reserved.

No part of this book may be reproduced, stored in a retrieval system, or transmitted in any form or by any means—electronic, mechanical, photocopying, recording, or otherwise—without prior written permission from the author.

Printed in the United States of America.

Published by Amazon KDP.

ISBN: 9798277130889

To the boy I used to be—

you carried pain no child should hold,

and you still kept going.

And to my parents—

your loops became my lessons,

your love became my compass,

and your absence became my awakening

What you repeat becomes who you are – until awareness breaks the loop.

CHAPTER 1

Born In Loops

"You're worthless. Pick up your goddamn feet. Why don't you go live with the trash on the south side?"

Those words from my stepdad still echo in my head.

I never knew which version of him I'd get. The sound of his footsteps coming down the stairs at night filled me with pure fear. Would he burst in and scream, or disappear back into the kitchen?

My mom was the only one brave enough to stand between us when he was drunk and angry. She was my buffer, my safety. When she was out of town, the fear set in deeper. She wasn't there to govern his drinking—or his rage.

He was a monster of a man with a stare that could pierce a room. If you got that look, you shut up or faced his wrath. He ruled our house with fear, the same way he'd been raised—anger and control without tenderness. Outside the house he was charming—funny, magnetic—but once the front door shut, the mask dropped. Inside those walls, he was a monster.

My mom was my rock—my best friend, my mama bear.

She'd battled alcoholism and addiction young. Both of her parents were alcoholics, so her path made sense. She got sober the day she walked out of the bathroom after shooting up and saw me and my sister hiding under the kitchen table, terrified. That image snapped her awake. She changed—for us, but more importantly, for herself.

She stayed sober for most of my life. I couldn't have handled it if all my parents had been alcoholics. She fought hard to become who she needed to be.

Then one day they called us into the living room. I was in sixth grade, watching a video about cancer. My rock—the woman who protected my life—was now fighting for hers.

I had never seen strength like hers. Not the kind that lifts weight—the kind that lifts people.

She had unshakable faith, mental fortitude, and a peace that inspired everyone around her. She'd look me in the eyes and say, "Son, I'm going to be okay. I'm in God's hands. This too shall pass."

She's where I learned most of my constructive loops.
She did aerobics three times a week, ate clean, traveled, loved skiing, journaled, meditated every morning. No matter what life threw at her, she stayed positive. She was in and out of hospitals constantly—every visit a life-or-death scenario—and I lived in constant fear of losing her. But her faith carried her through every storm. Her strength became my blueprint for survival—proof that loops can build as powerfully as they destroy.

My dad was a good man, but alcohol owned him too. He tried to get sober, but that loop dragged him down until it took his life.

As a kid, I cried over it—couldn't understand why he didn't love me enough to quit. Wasn't I worth it? Why did I get stuck with an abusive stepdad when all I wanted was my dad to be there?

Eventually I saw what alcohol did to him. The fun, party guy turned into a man who couldn't go a moment without vodka in his orange juice. He tried to show up, but the bottle kept pulling him under—DWIs, living out of his truck, always running from himself.

Then came the call: "If there's anything you want to say to your dad, you better get here—he's dying."

When I arrived, the strong man who'd climbed telephone poles for decades was gone—yellow skin, frail body, shaking from withdrawal. I thought it was the end. But somehow he fought back. He strung together five years of sobriety—the best version of my dad I ever knew. He raised my niece like a second chance, first in line every day to pick her up, proud of everything she did.

Then his loop crept back in. It started with "just a beer" and ended the way it always did—full relapse.

The last time we spoke, he'd flipped his truck with my niece in the back seat. I asked if he'd been drinking. He lied. I asked again, told him to swear on my life. He lied again.

I stopped talking to him after that. Six months later, he was gone.

No goodbye. No one more "I love you."
Just gone.

By forty, all three of my parents were gone—each taken by their own loops.

I didn't grow up with a model for healthy love or a healthy life.

I didn't know it then, but everything—the drinking, the anger, the fear, the faith, the hope—were loops repeating themselves, generation after generation, shaping me long before I had words for them.

This book is about those loops—
the ones that build us,
the ones that break us,
and the ones that, if we're brave enough to face them, set us free.

CHAPTER 2

What is a Loop

I'm not a scientist or a psychologist.
I'm just a man who's walked through valleys of pain, climbed mountains of loss, and swum through seas of heartbreak and self-destruction — and somehow made it out the other side.

This book isn't written in clinical jargon or theory.
It's built from experience, distilled into a framework that explains why we behave the way we do — and how we can finally change it.

Everything in existence moves in repetition.
Every breath, every heartbeat, every sunrise, every season.
In physics, it's called a cycle.
In nature, a rhythm.
In you, a loop.

A loop is anything that returns to itself — a feedback pattern where output becomes input and creates the next moment.
It's how energy moves, how life learns, and how you become who you are.

You wake up thinking a certain thought, feel a certain way, take a certain action, and that action reinforces the same thought.
That's a loop — the mind repeating itself until awareness interrupts it.

Nature works the same way: water evaporates, rises, falls, and returns to the ocean.
Stars form, burn, collapse, and seed new stars.
Nothing in existence is a straight line; everything curves back into itself to continue the flow.

The Flower of Life

Long before anyone had words for energy, vibration, or frequency, ancient civilizations carved the same pattern into stone — a web of overlapping circles known as the Flower of Life.
It appears everywhere: etched into the granite walls of the Temple of Osiris in Egypt, carved into temples in China, inscribed within the ruins of Turkey, and mirrored in Hindu mandalas and Hebrew Kabbalah.

These cultures were separated by oceans, centuries, and language — yet they all preserved the same design.
No shared communication. No shared religion. Just the same geometry repeating itself across the planet.

That's not coincidence. That's recognition.

They saw what modern science is only now rediscovering — that everything in existence moves in cycles, connects through patterns, and builds through repetition.
The Flower of Life wasn't decoration; it was a map — a visual equation of how the universe expands, contracts, and renews itself in perfect rhythm.

Ancient humanity already understood what we're remembering now: our lives run in loops, our choices overlap like circles, and together they form the same pattern that shapes galaxies, atoms, and time itself.

Loops in You

When you strip life down — habits, addictions, routines, trauma, conditioning — everything circles back to loops.
They're the invisible scripts running in the background of your mind, shaping every thought, action, and emotion.

Your morning routine? Loop.
Your reaction when someone cuts you off in traffic? Loop.
The relationship you can't let go of? Loop.

Our lives are woven from repeating patterns of thought, emotion, and behavior.
Some lift us — fueling growth and love.

Others suffocate us — anchoring us to fear, guilt, addiction, and pain.

But here's the truth: you're not broken.
You're just running code written before you knew you had a choice.

Your parents had loops. Their parents did too.
Society, culture, religion — these are loops we mistake for truth simply because they repeat.

Imagine walking the same path through tall grass every day.
Over time, a trail forms — easy, automatic, predictable.
That's what a loop does in your brain. It carves deep neural grooves that make old behaviors feel natural.

That's why we call it second nature.
You don't have to think about how to brush your teeth or drive your car — you've walked that path through the grass so many times that your brain performs the loop automatically, without conscious thought.

Your brain isn't judging; it's conserving energy.
It doesn't care if a loop is healthy or destructive — it just runs the program.

Over time, these loops shape your identity. They dictate how you love, how you react, how you see yourself and the world.
They're not destiny — they're conditioning. And once you see them, you can change them.

That's the purpose of this book: to recognize the loops that govern your life and take back control.
Once you understand the framework, you'll see how your personal loops intertwine with family, community, and even the patterns of the universe itself.

The Mechanics of a Loop
T → B → R → B

Every loop — addiction, anger, fear, kindness, love — runs the same universal code:

Trigger → Behavior → Reward → Belief

Trigger: the spark — anything from a text to a memory.
Behavior: the reaction — fight, flight, scroll, drink, hide, perform.
Reward: the payoff — relief, validation, escape.
Belief: the cement — the mind whispers, "See? That worked." The loop locks in.

The Language of Loops

Dopamine — "Happy Juice." Motivation and pursuit. Too much and you chase addiction; balanced and you chase purpose.

Serotonin — "Peace Serum." Built by sunlight, gratitude, and rhythm. Low levels fuel anxiety and depression loops.

Oxytocin — "Trust Glue." Formed through touch, eye contact, and connection — the foundation of emotional safety.

Cortisol — "Stress Signal." Vital in small doses, destructive in excess. Chronic stress equals loop overload.

The Nervous System. Your sympathetic system is the accelerator; your parasympathetic is the brake.
Balance is mastery. The vagus nerve — the peace wire — links mind and body, slowing the heart and stabilizing emotion.

Constructive vs. Destructive Loops

Constructive loops build life — gratitude, discipline, love, peace.

Destructive loops erode it — fear, anger, avoidance, addiction.

The goal isn't to escape the loop.
It's to understand it.

The loop you ignore becomes your cage.
The loop you study becomes your compass.

CHAPTER 3

The Mirror

I used to believe that if I got far enough or successful enough, I could outrun the chaos I came from.

But pain doesn't disappear—it waits.

It hides in the corners of your mind until life hands you a mirror big enough to see what you've become.

For years, I chased the version of myself I thought the world wanted—loud, confident, bulletproof.

Money, alcohol, adrenaline, validation.
On the surface, I looked alive.
Underneath, I was running from a scared kid who still remembered his stepdad's boots on the stairs.

My loops were already in motion.

The same fear that kept me quiet as a kid kept me performing as an adult.
If I could be liked, I'd be safe.
If I could impress, I'd be loved.
If I could rescue others, maybe someone would finally rescue me.

Every "yes" I gave to things that weren't good for me was really a "no" to myself.

I said yes to the party, yes to the drink, yes to the girl who needed saving—because it felt familiar.

Familiar isn't healthy; it's just known.

And when your nervous system confuses chaos with comfort, you keep choosing it.

People call it addiction—alcohol, sex, validation—but it's deeper than that: I was addicted to my loops.

Every destructive choice was an attempt to replay an old script and get a different ending.

But the ending never changed—until I did.

Heartbreak. Hangovers. Loss.
Each one blamed on fate or someone else.

Until one day, I stopped.
I looked in the mirror—really looked—and saw every version of me staring back:

The child. The addict. The charmer. The survivor.

All of them trapped in the same loop, waiting for me to wake up.

That's when it hit me:
Every loop has a lesson.
And until you learn it, you'll keep living it.

You can switch partners, jobs, cities, or vices—but the pattern follows until you face it.

That's why they say, "Wherever you go, there you are."
It's not cliché—it's law.

So I made a decision:
To stop running and start reflecting.
To understand that awareness is the first step to freedom.

Because when you stop blaming the world and start observing your patterns, you realize the villain was never fate, luck, or love.
It was the unconscious loops running the show all along.

And the moment you see them—truly see them—
that's when healing begins.

CHAPTER 4

The Ego Meltdown

The months leading up to Burning Man were the darkest of my life.

First, I lost my dog — my best friend, my road partner, my heartbeat. She wasn't just a pet; she was my shadow, my protector, and the one soul who never judged me no matter how broken I was. She'd sit next to me through every hangover, every heartbreak, every night I didn't think I'd make it. When everyone else left, she stayed.
She made me feel like no matter how chaotic life got, there was still one safe place left on earth — right next to her.

She went in for surgery, and the vet called to tell me she was fine — recovering well. I slept that night thinking she'd be home soon.
The next morning, they called to tell me she had died in the middle of the night, and they didn't know why.

It shattered my world.
All I could think about was her being scared and trapped in a cage, wondering where I was, when all she ever wanted was to be lying next to me. Once again, I didn't get to say goodbye. Didn't get to love on her one last time.

I didn't just lose my dog. I lost the one living being who embodied unconditional love in its purest form. The silence after was deafening.

☐

Three months later, my mom passed away — the strongest woman I've ever known, my anchor, my rock, my source of faith and reason.

She had fought cancer for years with a grace I still can't comprehend. Even when her body was failing, her spirit refused to break. She used to tell me, "You can find light in any darkness, son. You just have to look hard enough."

She was the one who taught me how to love, how to persevere, how to believe in something greater than myself. She believed in me when no one else did, not even me.

No matter what, my mom was always there.
Through the principal meetings, the court appearances, the rehab stints, the prison sentence — no matter how far I fell, she never stopped showing up for me.
Until she couldn't.

There's a kind of pain that doesn't scream — it hums quietly under your skin. That's what losing her felt like.
I'd wake up reaching for my phone to call her, only to remember she wasn't there.
The woman who taught me how to live was gone, and all I could think was: How am I supposed to do this without her?

☐

A month after that, my girlfriend — the person I had leaned on through the chaos — cheated on me.
I found out in a way that stripped every last illusion I had left.

After losing my dog and my mom, I thought there couldn't possibly be anything left to take — but heartbreak proved me wrong. It wasn't just betrayal; it was confirmation of every loop I'd been running my whole life — trust, lose, repeat.
It reopened every wound I thought had scarred over.
Love had always been the one place I thought I could find peace, and suddenly even that felt poisoned.

In the span of four months, everyone who meant everything to me was gone.
My world collapsed into silence.

☐

So when I headed to Burning Man, I wasn't looking for enlightenment — I was looking for escape.
I didn't care about spiritual awakenings or transformation. I just wanted to stop feeling.
I thought if I could drown out the noise long enough, maybe I could forget how bad it hurt.

The desert felt like another planet — a place suspended between heaven and hell.
Music pounded through the dust, lights shimmered against the black horizon, and people danced like their pain couldn't find them out there.
But mine did.

I was surrounded by thousands and had never felt more alone.
That's when it hit — not a wave, but a flood.
Every ounce of guilt, shame, anger, and regret I had ever buried erupted all at once.
It wasn't gentle. It was violent.

I collapsed in the back of my van, curled into the fetal position, shaking, sobbing, begging God to make it stop.
It felt like every piece of armor I'd ever built was being ripped off one layer at a time — all the masks, all the stories, all the lies I told myself to survive.

What I thought was a bad trip was actually an ego death — the total collapse of who I thought I was.
It was terrifying. It was raw.
But in that darkness, something deeper was trying to break through.

It felt like dying.
But something ancient and true was being reborn.

◻

When the sun rose the next morning, the world looked the same — but I didn't.
It was like waking up from a dream I didn't know I'd been living in.
The illusion of control was gone.
The illusion of identity was gone.
All that was left was awareness — naked, unfiltered, honest.

I could finally see my loops for what they were.
The addictions, the chasing, the rescuing, the performing — none of it was random.
It was my ego trying to protect a scared inner child that had never healed.
Every drink, every argument, every impulsive choice was just my pain trying to prove it was still alive.

The desert stripped me bare.

It forced me to face the truth that all the destruction I blamed on others was really my own reflection.
It wasn't a spiritual awakening in the cliché sense.
It was an unmaking — an emotional demolition.

That night in the desert wasn't my breakdown.
It was the beginning of my awakening.

When I left Burning Man, I didn't drive home.
I drove into the wild.
My instincts pulled me straight to nature — the only place that felt safe enough to process what I had just lived through.
The forest. The rivers. The silence.
Where the noise of the world couldn't reach me — and for the first time, I could finally start to hear myself again.

CHAPTER 5

The Break that Opened Everything

We met when I was living in California.
I thought she was the most beautiful girl I'd ever seen. We hung out a few times, but our loops never seemed to sync — we were living two completely different lives at the time.

Fifteen years later, we reconnected by accident — a rogue social-media message I sent without meaning to.
Could this be fate?
Could the girl I used to be obsessed with finally be mine?

I felt like it was destiny. Like the universe knew how lonely I was and decided to put her in my path to save me.

I finally thought this was my chance to have my person — my soulmate.
Everything on the outside seemed so perfect.
We were just alike. We had the same struggles growing up. We were both sober. She was an amazing mother and deeply connected to her family.

From the start, it was magic.
Since we lived in different states, every time we saw each other we created incredible memories in short bursts — skydiving in Maui, hiking and camping at Havasu Falls, rope-swinging in Moab.
I finally felt like I'd found the person I was meant to share my life with.

But slowly, the push and pull began.
One week she'd tell me I was everything she ever wanted; the
next, she'd disappear for days without a word — then return as if nothing had happened, pulling me right back in.
I told myself this was love — that passion and chaos were the same thing.
But deep down, I knew something was off.

Then one morning, she sent me a photo of a pregnancy test.
Positive.

I was flooded with emotion — fear, joy, hope, confusion.

We had always talked about having a child and building a family together.
I thought this was it — the moment everything would finally make sense.

But just as quickly as it came, she was gone.
Silence.
No answers.

When she finally resurfaced, she said she wanted to make it work.
And like a fool, I believed her.
We planned a week with the kids, and I drove four states away to see her — desperate to believe that love could fix anything, that maybe this time would be different.

But within days, the same arguments started.
She pushed, I tried to reason, and soon she told me to get out of her house.
And just like that, I was back in the same cycle — confused, hurt, abandoned.

Then she said the words that changed everything:
"If I'm so horrible, why do you always come back?"

The question hit me like a freight train.
Why did I keep coming back?
Why was I addicted to my own pain?

That single sentence echoed in my head for days until it cracked something open in me that I could never close again.

I wanted to run home — but I was miles away.
And something inside me whispered: Stop running.
Running had been my loop all along.

So instead, I drove into the forest and sat in the silence.
No phone. No noise.
Just me and my thoughts.

I decided to feel every ounce of the pain I'd spent years avoiding — the loneliness, the rejection, the endless cycle of trying to fix people who didn't want to be fixed.

Something in me said, find a book to listen to — anything to calm the storm.
I scrolled aimlessly, and the first title that appeared was It's Not You: Healing from Narcissistic Abuse.
It felt divine.

I hit play.

As I listened, I started to see patterns — loops — unfolding right before me.
Every story mirrored mine almost perfectly: the love-bombing, the future-faking, the devaluation, the discard.
Different people, same sequence.

One of the key takeaways from that book hit me like lightning:
"A narcissist will never change. No matter what — they don't change."

That sentence cracked something open in my mind.
Is she really just living life on autopilot — repeating the same behaviors over and over, completely unaware of the destruction she's causing?
How could anyone with a conscience treat someone that way and still genuinely believe it wasn't their fault?

But then it hit me — I was the exact same way.

I never let a woman get too close.
I always kept them at arm's length, using them for whatever I needed in the moment — validation, comfort, distraction.
I did it for years, convincing myself I was in control.
But after my experience at Burning Man, I started to see my loops.

I saw how my combination of childhood loops, peer and school loops, and societal loops had all led me to that very point in my life.
I didn't see myself as a monster or a bad person — but my behaviors were destructive and hurtful all the same.
That's why I kept dating the same woman over and over, and why I kept getting the same result.

Then came the realization that changed everything:
If she was on a loop, and I was on a loop — who else was?

That's when it hit me.
We all are.

Everyone is running loops — some conscious, most not.
We're all walking around, repeating the same day over and over, reacting to the same triggers, falling into the same cycles, thinking we're making choices — when in reality, we're just following programming.

The programming can come from anywhere: parents, peers, religion, media, trauma, culture.
But until you become aware of it, it runs on autopilot — looping endlessly in your mind, directing your life from the shadows.

That was the day I realized I'm not a victim or a survivor.
I experience life and react — but now I can observe it.
And when you reach that place of awareness, you start to see that everyone and everything around you is just running on unconscious loops.

That's when I understood something simple but undeniable: it was never bad luck that I kept ending up with the same kind of partner and the same kind of pain — it was math.
Run the same formula, get the same result.
Change the variables — change the outcome.
If I could shift my loops and recognize the loops in others, I could rewrite the equation and change the entire trajectory of my life.

I'm not condoning child abuse, but my stepdad didn't beat me because he hated me or because there was something wrong with me — he did it because he was running on the programming of destructive loops.
My ex didn't emotionally torture me or berate me because of my loops — she was just running on her own survival autopilot.

Once I understood that, I stopped seeing enemies and started seeing patterns.
Pain turned into perspective.
Judgment turned into understanding.
And with that awareness, everything began to change.

I sat there in the forest for hours — no phone, no noise, no distractions.
Just the sound of the wind through the trees, the steady rhythm of the river beside me, and the realization that even nature runs on loops.
The tides, the seasons, the growth and decay — all of it repeating, all of it balanced.
The same intelligence that guides the forest was guiding me.

That was the day I stopped trying to control everything and became the observer — the day I realized life isn't about breaking loops; it's about understanding them.

And right there, in the stillness of that forest — where everything just was — Loop Theory was born.

CHAPTER 6

The Awakening

The forest was silent — but it wasn't empty.
The wind moved through the trees like breath through lungs, and for the first time in years, I wasn't trying to escape the silence. I was listening to it.

I sat there with swollen eyes and a heavy body, but inside, something finally stilled.
The river nearby wasn't background noise anymore; it was rhythm — a loop. Each ripple flowed forward without resistance, never questioning where it was meant to go.

Then it hit me.
Everything around me moved in cycles — loops written into the fabric of existence.
The trees shed and regrow their leaves.
The tides rise and fall in rhythm with the moon.
The sun rises, sets, and returns — without fail.
Birds migrate the same paths across the sky.
Wolves howl in cadence with one another.
Even the river beside me repeats itself — the same water that leaves eventually finds its way back through clouds and rain.
Life breathes in patterns.

And for the first time, I saw the connection: we're no different.
Humans are loops too.

All the heartbreaks, losses, and anger — none of it was random. It was the collision of programs.
My loops.
Her loops.
The generational loops passed down before either of us ever had a choice.
Every destructive pattern in my life was just old code no one had stopped to question.

I thought back to that relationship — the love-bombing, the chaos, the constant push and pull.
I had believed she was my soulmate.
She was my mirror — reflecting everything in me that still needed healing.

That realization broke me open.
All those years, I thought I was cursed, unlucky in love, even the problem.
But in that forest I understood: it wasn't me, and it wasn't her.
It was our loops.

She pulled away when things got good — not because she didn't care, but because abandonment was her loop.
I chased and over-proved my worth — not because it was love, but because unworthiness was mine.
We weren't loving each other; we were reenacting pain.

That's when the truth landed: you can't change anyone else's loops — only your own.
You control how you show up, how you respond, and whether you continue the pattern or end it.

In that stillness, I became the observer.
It was like stepping out of the program and finally seeing the code.
I could trace every loop that ran my life — fear, guilt, shame, addiction, validation — each pretending to keep me safe.

That's where healing began.
Heartbreak softened.
Loss started to make sense.
It wasn't punishment; it was alignment.
Every collision was trying to wake me up — to teach, refine, and bring me back to balance.
It's not enough to see your loops — you have to interrupt them.
Every time you pause before reacting, breathe instead of breaking, choose understanding over anger — you're rewriting code.
That's how transformation happens: one conscious choice at a time.

That day in the forest, I stopped surviving my loops.
I started mastering them.
And for the first time in my life, I wasn't running from the program — I was rewriting it.

CHAPTER 7

The Geometry of Life

I couldn't stop seeing it — patterns everywhere. Repetition. Order hiding inside what I used to call chaos.

It wasn't just in the woods. It was life itself.
Morning alarms. Coffee at the same time. The same route to work. The same arguments, the same triggers, the same distractions.
We wake, run the same programs, and call it living.
Loops stacked on loops — programming disguised as personality.

Then I saw the same thing in nature — but nature doesn't resist its loops.
It flows through them.
Trees don't cling to their leaves in winter.
Oceans don't argue with the moon.
Fire doesn't apologize for burning.
Nature adapts, releases, renews, and moves forward through rhythm.

Everything follows a pattern:
the trees shedding and regrowing their leaves,
the tides rising and falling with the moon,
the sun rising and setting with precision,
plants exhaling oxygen, animals returning carbon, rivers cycling water through cloud and rain.

Even your own body obeys the same intelligence.
Your lungs expand and contract like tides.
Your circadian rhythm mirrors Earth's rotation.
Your heart beats in repeating intervals like a drum inside a much larger song.
The same loops that guide the oceans guide you.

Life doesn't move in straight lines; it spirals — expanding, contracting, evolving each time it returns.
You can see that spiral everywhere: in the unfurling of a fern, the swirl of a hurricane, the arms of a galaxy, even the double helix of your DNA.

It's the same blueprint — a repeating ratio that builds life itself.

That ratio — 1.618, the Golden Ratio — is the fingerprint of creation.
It's nature's architecture, hidden in plain sight.
It determines how leaves turn toward light, how sunflowers pack their seeds, how storms rotate, how galaxies spin.
It shapes seashells, pinecones, hurricanes — and you.
It's not random. It's math.

Even beauty itself echoes it.
Faces, art, and music that feel balanced follow the same proportion.
We literally feel harmony when we see the code that built us.

If you want to understand loops, watch a dog.
You reach for the leash — the click of metal is the trigger.
Instantly the tail wags, dopamine floods, the body quivers — the behavior.
You open the door — the reward.
The mind locks it in: leash = walk = joy — the belief.
Now every sound of that leash runs the same program.

If that same dog was once struck, the pattern shifts.
A raised voice now means danger.
Trigger → Behavior → Reward → Belief still fires, only this time built from fear instead of love.
That's biology.
That's a loop.

We're no different.
Our nervous systems run the same code — just with fancier toys.
Your phone buzzes (trigger).
You grab it before thinking (behavior).
A like or comment hits (reward).
Your brain whispers, See? I matter. (belief).

Only difference?
Your leash is your phone.
Your treat is a like.
Your "good boy" is a heart emoji.

Dog treats are our social-media likes.
Different species, same chemistry — both chasing the same molecule of belonging.

Every swipe, every scroll, every refresh cuts a deeper path through your neural grass.
You're not broken; you're conditioned.
The same survival loop that once kept you alive in the wild now keeps you trapped in the feed.

But there's another layer — one that changed how I see everything alive.

We think we're advanced because we built Wi-Fi.
Trees have been doing it for millions of years.

Beneath every forest lies a living web of fungi — the mycorrhizal network — connecting trees, plants, and entire ecosystems.
Scientists call it the Wood Wide Web.
Through it, trees send nutrients to their young, warn neighbors of disease, and even "decide" which plants to support or starve.
An old tree can feed a younger tree miles away.
A dying tree can release its stored carbon to help its forest survive.
Nothing is isolated. Everything is connected.

This isn't mysticism; it's measurable biology.
It's feedback loops at work on a scale so vast and so elegant we're only beginning to comprehend it.
The same intelligence that organizes your neurons organizes the forest floor.
The same feedback that regulates your heartbeat regulates the flow of carbon beneath your feet.
The forest breathes as one organism — a living loop of give and take.

Once I saw that, it was impossible not to see the pattern everywhere.
From fungus and roots to storms and stars, the universe runs on recursion — self-repeating, self-correcting, endlessly refining.

Tesla said, "If you want to find the secrets of the universe, think in terms of energy, frequency, and vibration."
He was right.
Energy moves in waves.
Waves repeat in frequency.
Frequency sustains vibration.
Vibration forms matter.
Matter becomes life.
And life returns that energy back into the field.

Everything is cycling — from electrons around atoms to planets around suns to galaxies around black holes.
Each motion is a loop.
Each loop, a conversation of energy returning to its source.

This isn't philosophy; it's physics.
Your thoughts pulse in electrical waves.
Your heart emits measurable electromagnetic fields.
Every action, word, and emotion sends a frequency outward that interacts with others.
Your personal energy isn't contained — it's participating in the same universal circuit that powers stars.

That's the realization that changes everything:
Your loops aren't separate from the universe's loops.
They are the same process, scaled differently.

Your anxiety, habits, heartbreaks — none of it is random punishment.
It's feedback from the same system that moves tides, seasons, and galaxies.
Every destructive loop in your life isn't there to ruin you; it's there to refine you.
Every collision is data, showing you where you're out of sync with the larger pattern.

When your internal frequency is chaotic — fear, guilt, anger — you vibrate out of tune with the system and feel that dissonance as struggle.
When you align — gratitude, awareness, love — you move back into resonance.
Your personal loops harmonize with nature's rhythm.
Life stops feeling like resistance and starts feeling like flow.

Nothing in nature resists flow.
A fallen tree becomes soil.
Decay feeds growth.
Predators and prey sustain balance.
Even death nourishes new life.
Nothing is wasted. Nothing stands alone.

Humans are the only species that tries to step outside this design — to control, hoard, dominate.
We disconnect from the loop and call it progress, then wonder why we feel lost.
We're not cursed; we're just out of sync.

But once you understand the loop, you can step back in.
You can rewrite the equation.
Change the variable, change the outcome.
Awareness is the variable.
Conscious choice is the variable.
That's how you change the trajectory of your life.

Life doesn't evolve by chance; it evolves by iteration.
Each loop carries the lessons of the last — just like you do.
Every time you pause before reacting, breathe instead of breaking, choose understanding over anger — you're rewriting your code and syncing with the larger code of existence.

When I finally understood that, the boundaries between self, nature, and cosmos disappeared.
I wasn't separate from the design.
I was the design.
So are you.

You're not here to escape the system.
You're here to remember that you are the system — a living, breathing, looping expression of the same intelligence that moves the tides and spins the stars.

Once you see that, you stop trying to control life.
You start moving with it — perfectly in rhythm.

CHAPTER 8

The Observer

For most of my life, I lived inside the storm.
Every thought, emotion, and reaction tossed me around like debris in a hurricane.
One text, one careless comment, one flash of memory — that's all it took to send me spiraling.
I didn't realize it then, but I was trapped in loops of my own mind — replaying old stories, defending wounds, reacting to ghosts.

When I discovered Loop Theory, everything began to shift.
I started noticing patterns — not just in others, but in myself.
Life was never happening to me; it was happening through me.
I was the one feeding the loops, keeping the storm alive with every thought, every reaction, every burst of anger or fear.

Then one day, something inside me just ... stopped.
The noise broke.
I remember sitting in silence, feeling this strange distance between my thoughts and me.
For the first time, I wasn't lost in the chaos — I was watching it.

That's when I realized: I can be the Observer instead of the participant.
Life isn't happening to you — it's happening around you.

When you become the Observer, you stop being tossed by the storm of your thoughts, emotions, and reactions.
You step into the eye — the still, unshakable center.
The chaos keeps swirling — people, triggers, heartbreaks, responsibilities — but it no longer owns you.
From that still point, you can watch without drowning, choose without being hijacked, and respond instead of react.
That's where your power lives.
That's freedom.

In that instant — the split second before you react — you have a choice.
That's the space where the Observer lives.

Someone cuts you off in traffic.
Before you can think, you're screaming — but they're not hearing it. You are.
Your heart races, cortisol floods.
That's not anger; that's your nervous system running old code.
When you pause, breathe, and choose not to react, you step outside the loop.
You rise above the pattern.

Think of the Flower of Life.
Each circle represents a loop — emotions, habits, people, experiences — overlapping to create the geometry of existence.
When you live unconsciously, you're trapped inside those circles, colliding and repeating.
But the moment you pause, you step into the space between them — the still point that connects everything yet belongs to nothing.
That's the eye of the storm.
That's awareness.
That's you — the observer standing between worlds.

And in that space, you're free.

Most people spend their lives as participants.
They chase happiness, fight pain, and try to control what's outside themselves.
But when you live as the Observer, the entire game changes.
You realize the only thing you truly control is your reaction — your loops.
Everything else is just weather passing through.

Being the Observer doesn't mean you stop feeling or caring.
It means you stop being controlled by what you feel.
When something or someone triggers you, instead of reacting, you pause.
Take a 3-6-9 breath.
Watch your emotions rise and fall like waves.
Notice the stories your mind tells.
See your loops reaching for autopilot — and choose not to follow.

That's awareness in real time — the moment between stimulus and response.
That tiny gap is the birthplace of freedom.

When you live as the Observer, life reveals itself as a flowing sequence of loops, intersecting and colliding all around you.

You see people acting out their programming — defensiveness, fear, jealousy, anger — and instead of judging, you understand.
Everyone is doing the best they can with the loops they were given.

When you realize that, judgment dissolves.
Blame disappears.
The storm calms.

You're no longer a victim of your past.
You're no longer trapped in cycles of pain.
You are the Observer.
You are awareness itself.
And awareness is the key that unlocks everything.

CHAPTER 9

The Ancestral Loop — Survival on Repeat

Long before phones, deadlines, and self-doubt, every human loop began the same way — survival.

Our ancestors weren't worried about emails or validation; they were worried about staying alive.
A rustle in the grass could mean a tiger. A flash of lightning could mean fire. That tension — that instant surge of alertness — is the same one you feel when your boss texts We need to talk.
Same code. New context.

Their bodies learned a rhythm that kept them alive:
Trigger → Reaction → Relief.
Hear danger. React fast. Survive.
The body rewarded them with a chemical cocktail — adrenaline, cortisol, dopamine — the same ones running through your veins right now.

We inherited that chemistry.
We're built from it.
But the brain never got the software update to tell the difference between a predator and a push notification.

That's why you check your phone a hundred times a day.
That's why you replay arguments, scroll headlines, wait for someone to text back.
Your biology is still trying to protect you from lions that no longer exist.

When food was scarce, hoarding meant survival.
Now it looks like overconsumption, binge-eating, greed.
When belonging meant safety from predators, rejection could be fatal.
Now it looks like social anxiety, comparison, or people-pleasing.

It's not weakness — it's wiring.
You're running ancient code on modern hardware.

But here's the twist: the same loops that once kept you alive can now keep you stuck.
The survival brain doesn't care if you're happy — only that you're alive.
It will push you toward familiar pain over unfamiliar peace,
because once, change meant danger.

That's why you stay in jobs you hate.
That's why you chase the same kind of partner.
That's why you repeat patterns even when you know they hurt.

Your nervous system confuses familiarity with safety.
It doesn't care if it's love or chaos — if it's predictable, it feels safe.
But safety isn't the same as peace.

We've evolved enough to build cities, rockets, and microchips —
but most of us are still reacting like cavemen.
The only difference?
The threats got smaller, but the reaction stayed the same.

You're not fighting a broken brain.
You're fighting evolution.

Awareness is the update our ancestors never had.
They couldn't see the loop. You can.
And the moment you can see it, you can change it.

You can teach your body that safety isn't out there anymore.
It's within you.
Every breath, every pause, every conscious choice tells your nervous system: We're not being chased anymore.

That's how healing begins — not by denying your primal wiring but by upgrading it.
You're not meant to erase your instincts; you're meant to evolve them.

Because awareness isn't rebellion against biology.
It's the next step of evolution itself.

You're carrying thousands of years of survival in your skin.
Every instinct, every fear, every urge to run began as protection.
But the world has changed.

And for the first time in human history, you have the awareness to see the loop as it's happening.

Your ancestors didn't get that choice.
You do.

You can stop running.
You can breathe.
You can choose differently.

Maybe that's what evolution has been building toward all along —
not a stronger body,
but a conscious mind.
Not the instinct to survive,
but the wisdom to finally live.

CHAPTER 10

The Shaping of You

Before you ever made a single conscious choice, life was already programming you.
Every cry that was answered — or ignored.
Every tone of voice, slammed door, or bedtime story.
Each one carved a pathway in your nervous system.
Your mind learned what brought safety and what brought pain, and it built loops to survive both.

If your mom screamed when she was overwhelmed, you have the same explosions of anger and frustration.
If your dad gave you attention only when you achieved something, you learned that love must be earned.
If affection was rare, you learned to chase it.
If chaos was constant, calm felt foreign.
These patterns didn't form because you were weak; they formed because your body was smart.
It built automatic responses — loops — to keep you alive in whatever world you were born into.

As a child, you mirrored the people you depended on.
When your parents couldn't regulate their emotions, you learned to scream and throw tantrums by watching it.
When they shut down, you learned to withdraw.
When they distracted themselves, you learned avoidance.
That's how loops pass from one generation to the next — not through DNA, but through behavior modeled day after day until it becomes identity.

By the time you hit adulthood, you've walked those mental trails so many times that they've turned into highways.
You react before you think.
You explain your actions with stories like "That's just who I am," when in truth, it's just who you were taught to be.

Your "personality" is a mosaic of survival patterns layered over time — humor that hides fear, confidence that masks shame, independence that protects you from ever needing anyone again.

But here's the moment everything changes:
Once you see the code, you can rewrite it.
Awareness cracks the surface.
Every time you notice a trigger and pause instead of reacting, you're cutting a new path through the grass.
Every time you breathe instead of break, you teach your body that it's safe again.

You start to see how much of your life has been a repetition of someone else's pain.
That's not self-blame — it's liberation.
Because if you were programmed, you can be re-programmed.

The Undoing of the Mask

When that realization hits, it can shake you to your core.
You start asking yourself, Who would I be if I stopped trying to be everything for everyone else?
If I didn't have to keep the peace, fix everyone's problems, or always be the strong one — who am I, really?

It's a scary question because those versions of you were built for survival.
You learned to read the room before you could even read words.
You adjusted your tone, your behavior, your emotions — all to stay safe, accepted, or loved.
Those habits kept you alive, but they also kept you from ever truly being seen.

You don't have to force anything or "find yourself" overnight.
Just start noticing.
When you catch yourself slipping into an old pattern, pause and ask:
Is this me — or is this what I learned to be?

That question is everything.
That's where awareness lives.
Each time you ask it, a little more of the real you steps forward.

You don't need to reinvent yourself — you just need to remember who you were before the world told you who to be.
That's how the unlearning begins — not in some grand awakening, but in quiet moments of honesty.

The truth is — you were never broken.
You were just programmed.
And now, for the first time, you finally have the power to reprogram yourself.

CHAPTER 11

The Loops We Live

Once you see how you were shaped, you start noticing the patterns everywhere — in your thoughts, your routines, the way you talk to yourself when no one's listening.
It's like someone finally turned the lights on, and you realize your life has been running on a series of loops — every emotion, reaction, and decision connected by invisible threads you never saw before.

The beautiful part?
Now that you're aware, you hold the power to change them.

Because it's not just the big moments that define your life — it's the small ones.
The coffee you reach for, the thoughts you feed, the habits you repeat without question.
Those micro-loops stack up day after day until they shape your reality.

So before we talk about love, heartbreak, and the way your loops collide with others, we need to look at how they move through you — every hour, every choice, every breath.
Let's step into your day and see what's really running the show.

The Time Loop

People always say, "I don't have time."
But the truth is, we do — we just hand it over to autopilot.

The average person spends more than two hours a day scrolling — feeds, stories, videos, likes — and another couple watching shows.
That's roughly four hours every day spent consuming instead of creating.

Four hours a day is twenty-eight a week.
Over a year, that's roughly sixty full days of your life — two entire months, gone.

People don't run out of time; they fall asleep to it.
Autopilot doesn't steal your hours all at once — it takes them one scroll, one episode, one funny video or one "next time" at a time.

Imagine redirecting just half that time — two hours a day — into constructive loops: reading, journaling, exercising, learning, building, loving.
You could master a skill, rebuild your body, or change the trajectory of your life in a single year.

You do have time.
You've just been asleep at the wheel.

You're not broken.
You're just running on old loops — ones handed to you, programmed into you, or burned into your nervous system by survival.
Every thought, habit, and reaction you have today is a reflection of those loops.
They kept you alive once, but now they're keeping you stuck.

Now that you've stepped into the role of the Observer, you hold the power to rewrite every single one.
This is where your life either stays the same — or changes forever.

Perfection isn't the goal.
Direction is.
You don't need to erase every flaw or master every habit overnight.
You just need to start replacing destructive loops with constructive ones — one decision at a time — so the trajectory of your life finally begins to spiral upward instead of down.

Because if you keep doing what you've always done, your life will look exactly the same in five, ten, twenty years.
If you're miserable at your job and do nothing, it won't fix itself.
If your relationship feels like two strangers under one roof, that
spark won't reignite by chance.
If you keep numbing out each night and calling it rest, nothing will change.
Change doesn't come by waiting.
Change comes by breaking the loop.

This is your mirror.
Your call to action.
The wake-up alarm for your soul.

A Day in the Loops

Let's be brutally honest.
You wake up and grab your phone before your eyes even adjust to the light.
Dopamine hits — the first loop of the day.
You scroll, compare, feel behind.
Anxiety follows. Coffee to jolt the fatigue.
Fear disguised as responsibility keeps you chained to the job you hate.
Resentment disguised as routine shapes your relationship.
Numbness disguised as rest ends your night.

And tomorrow? You'll do it again.
Not because you want to — but because you're programmed to.
That's not living. That's surviving.
And surviving is just looping on life support.

The Brain's Default Setting

The brain craves efficiency. It's built for survival, not fulfillment.
Your brain works like water carving through canyons.
Every thought, reaction, and emotion is a flow that cuts a little deeper into the terrain of your mind.
Over time, those streams form neural pathways — routes your brain travels automatically.
Like water, your thoughts always follow the path of least resistance, even if that path leads somewhere destructive.
Soon, you're not choosing your reactions or thoughts — they're choosing you.
Your brain runs the code automatically.
That same mechanism keeps you locked in destructive habits — the same arguments, the same relationships, the same fears.
What started as a trickle of thoughts has become a flowing river of emotions.
That's why change feels uncomfortable at first — you're not broken, you're just redirecting the river

The Science of Autopilot

Every loop has chemistry behind it.
Cortisol spikes when you feel stress — even from checking your phone or sitting in traffic.
Dopamine floods when you scroll, drink, chase validation, or win an argument.

Your nervous system learns these rhythms like songs.
Feed it chaos, and it craves chaos.
Feed it peace, and it starts seeking peace.

You've heard the saying, "Time flies when you're having fun."
But time flies when you're unconscious.

When you're lost in loops, you stop noticing the details that make life worth living — the smell of rain, the warmth of sunlight, the quiet laughter of a stranger.
Ten years can vanish because you weren't there.
You were running code written decades ago.

That's why people stay stuck in jobs that drain them, relationships that suffocate them, and habits that quietly kill them — because the nervous system confuses familiar with safe.
Your comfort zone isn't a place; it's a collection of loops.
The mind would rather live in misery it understands than step into peace it can't predict.

Every loop, from heartbreak to habit, runs the same code:

Trigger → Behavior → Reward → Belief
Trigger: something happens — a text, a tone, a memory.
Behavior: you react — lash out, scroll, drink, shut down.
Reward: relief — dopamine, validation, escape. The brain says, That worked.
Belief: the cement. The mind whispers, Do that again next time.

You've just reinforced the code.
That's how loops build lives.

THE ALCOHOL LOOP: FROM ONE DRINK TO FULL DEPENDECE

1. Spark — The Innocent Beginning

Long day.
He wants to unwind.
He pours one drink to relax — completely normal.

Micro-relief hits:

stress drops
shoulders loosen
the mind quiets
dopamine rises

The nervous system learns:
"Drink → relief."

A loop seed is planted.

2. Pattern Formation — The First Circuit Closes

A few more nights: same trigger, same action.

Stress → alcohol → relief.

The brain records the chain and begins automating the response.

It's not addiction — it's a reinforced loop.
Trigger → Behavior → Reward → Reinforcement.

This is where the pattern becomes predictable.

3. Sleep Interference — The Loop Turns Destructive

Alcohol relaxes the mind early…
but fragments sleep later:

shallow REM
early waking
poor recovery

He wakes up groggy.

Groggy → more stress during the day → stronger urge to unwind at night.

The loop begins generating its own trigger.

The first destructive cycle appears:
Alcohol → bad sleep → more stress → more need for alcohol.

4. Emotional Shift — The Subtle Descent

Two things begin happening at the same time.

A. Subclinical depression creeps in

less energy
less motivation
more irritability
lower baseline mood

This isn't "depression" yet —
it's alcohol-driven emotional flattening.

B. Relief begins to feel necessary

He's not drinking to relax anymore.
He's drinking to feel normal.

The loop tightens.

5. Dependence Begins — The Loop Strengthens Itself

The body adapts.

Alcohol stops relaxing him like it used to.

So:

one drink becomes two
two becomes three

Not out of intention —
but because the loop now requires a higher dose to reach the same relief.

The loop becomes:
Stress → alcohol → partial relief → worse sleep → more stress → higher dose.

Drinking begins earlier in the evening,
sometimes even as a "reward" for getting through the day.

6. Identity Shift — When the Loop Becomes the Operator

This is the moment the loop evolves into identity.

He starts saying:

"I just like to drink at night."
"I unwind with a couple drinks."
"It's how I manage stress."

But now:

mood swings increase
cravings rise
drinking happens even on good days
emotional tolerance drops

The loop no longer waits for a trigger.
It runs on its own.

This is the shift from habit → pattern → identity.

7. Escalation Phase — Dependence to Early Alcoholism

The loop begins generating its own momentum:

sleep disruption intensifies
depression expands
mornings get harder
self-judgment rises
anxiety increases (especially after drinking)

He drinks to relieve the feelings
that the drinking itself created.

This is loop recursion.

The system becomes:
Alcohol → emotional instability → stronger cravings → more alcohol.

Alcohol becomes both the cause
and the attempted solution.

This is the hallmark of a destructive loop going critical.

8. Full-blown Alcoholism — When the Loop Runs the Life

Once enough cycles repeat, the loop becomes self-governing:

drinking earlier in the day
loss of control over quantity
needing alcohol to feel baseline
withdrawal between drinks
social or work impact
emotional numbing

isolation
shame → drinking to escape shame

At this stage, the loop is no longer just psychological —
it is physiological, emotional, behavioral, and identity-based.

The loop owns him until a major interruption occurs.

9. The Break — How Destructive Loops Finally Interrupt

Destructive alcohol loops break only through:

A. Hard contradiction

health scare
legal scare
partner intervention
losing something important
a "rock bottom" moment
a terrifying morning after

These shocks disrupt the loop long enough for clarity to break through.

B. Conscious interruption at the root

He interrupts the pattern before the first drink:

leaving the environment
changing the evening routine
regulating stress differently
addressing emotional load upstream

He changes the first step instead of waiting for the nightly trigger.

C. Identity shift

This is the deepest break.

When he stops seeing himself as
"someone who drinks to relax"

and becomes someone who regulates stress
through presence, breath, movement, or meaning.

Identity-level change kills the loop.

Why this case study matters

The alcohol loop reveals the full architecture of destructive loops:

tiny harmless beginning
positive reinforcement
hidden counter-effects
emotional drift
biological adaptation
identity integration
self-sustaining destruction
eventual collapse or interruption

This model applies to every destructive pattern humans fall into:

compulsive sex
toxic relationships
avoidance
anger cycles
self-sabotage
gambling
procrastination
binge eating
doom-scrolling
emotional withdrawal

The architecture is always the same.
Only the behavior on the surface changes.

This is Loop Theory in its rawest form —
the mechanics of how patterns become prisons.

Shifting the Formula

The loops you live aren't random — they're mathematical.
Input = Output.
You can't keep feeding the same equation and expect a different result.

Einstein said it best:
"The definition of insanity is doing the same thing over and over and expecting different results."

That's exactly what loops are — repeating the same actions, thoughts, and emotions, expecting life to somehow change.
But life doesn't change until you do.

Awareness gives you the power to alter the formula.
Change one variable — your reaction — and the entire outcome shifts.
That's not luck. That's physics.

Every moment of awareness is a chance to shift your trajectory.
Skip one drink.
Speak one truth.
Take one deep breath instead of exploding.
Walk outside instead of scrolling.
These are microscopic revolutions — the beginnings of constructive loops.

Rewriting My Own Code

In the past, I didn't use anger because I was strong. I used it because I didn't know what else to do. When something didn't go my way—business, relationships, even small interactions with strangers—I would snap. I'd raise my voice, press harder, overpower whoever was in front of me. It wasn't about the situation. It was about the feeling underneath it. Every time I felt blocked or dismissed, it pulled up the same old helplessness I carried from childhood. And I couldn't tolerate that feeling. I didn't know how to sit with it. So I'd override it with anger. Anger made me feel big for a moment, but only because I still felt so small inside. I wasn't fighting the person in front of me. I was fighting the boy who never felt like he had any power.

I don't want to be that person anymore.
I want to treat people with love and respect. Now I do something different.
When that trigger hits, I take a 3-6-9 breath — in for 3, hold for 6, out for 9 — and label it: my helplessness loop.
Just naming it takes away its power.
Ninety-nine percent of the time, they still can't help me — but at least I didn't lose myself.
I walk away calm, grounded, proud that I didn't let old programming run my new life.

That's how you rewrite your code.
Not by being perfect — but by being aware.
By choosing consciousness over reaction, breath over rage, grace over shame.

The Loops That Build You

You can't erase loops — they're how life operates.
But you can choose which ones you build.

Fear is a loop.
So is faith.
Addiction is a loop.
So is discipline.
Anger is a loop.
So is love.

Every choice either reinforces an old loop or builds a new one.
Stack enough constructive loops, and you'll watch your entire life bend upward.

The Call to Action

This is the part where you decide whether to wake up or go back to sleep.

If you hate your job — find a new one.
If your partner feels like a roommate — talk, reconnect, rebuild, or walk away.
If your habits are killing you — change them.

Stop waiting for the perfect moment. There isn't one.
The loops running your life don't care about your excuses — they only care about your repetition.

So break it.
Right here.
Right now.

Because this is the moment where the old you dies and the real you begins.
This is the day you stop existing on autopilot and start living with intention.

Your loops built your past.
Your awareness builds your future.

CHAPTER 12

The Human Heart Loop

You meet someone.
Instant spark.

Something about them feels magnetic — like gravity pulling two planets into orbit.
Your chest tightens, palms sweat, your heart races.
You can't explain it, but it feels meant to be.
They're your "type," your pattern — and your brain lights up like fireworks.

It's not fate.
It's feedback.

Your nervous system just recognized a familiar frequency.

The Pull — The Ignition Loop

At first, everything flows.
You talk for hours, laugh until it hurts, share secrets you've never spoken aloud.
They feel like home.

That's the chemistry of newness — dopamine and norepinephrine flooding your system, sharpening your focus, amplifying every moment.
Your brain makes the association: them = reward.
And that's how the loop begins.

But attraction isn't truth — it's tension.
That rush you call falling in love is your nervous system syncing with someone else's pattern.
Familiar doesn't mean healthy; it just means known.
And most people's "type" is simply their trauma wearing a different face.

The Bond — Merging Loops

Weeks turn into months.
You fall into rhythm.
Your texts, moods, even your sleep patterns sync.
You feel safe. Connected. Alive.

Biologically, you are.
Oxytocin and serotonin stabilize your system.
Your heartbeats literally begin to align when you hold each other.
Your nervous systems link into one shared loop — co-regulating safety and stress, like two instruments finding harmony.

But harmony can shift.
If one person starts to feel threatened, their system spikes — and the other follows.
Fear meets fear.
Defense meets defense.
You don't even realize you've stopped dancing and started reacting.

The Friction — Loops Colliding

It starts small — a comment that lands wrong, a text unanswered.
Your chest tightens. Your stomach drops.
Your attachment system flares: Something's wrong.

They pull away; you chase harder.
They go quiet; you spiral.
Both of you are running old survival codes — one wired to retreat, one wired to cling.

This is the collision point — where your childhood conditioning meets theirs.
Unless both of you see it, the loop runs until one of you breaks.

You start questioning yourself:
Why are we fighting so much?
Why can't they understand me?
Where did the person I fell in love with go?

Your body is exhausted; your mind numb.

You're not broken — your body thinks you're in danger.
Your nervous system has shifted from connection to survival.

Cortisol spikes. Digestion stalls. Sleep disappears.
You're not in love anymore — you're in defense.

The Collapse — The Breakup Loop

Then it ends.
Maybe suddenly, maybe slowly.
Either way, it feels like the ground disappears.

You can't eat. You can't sleep.
Every thought circles back to them.
Your body aches as if you've been physically wounded — because chemically, you have.

When love breaks, the circuits that once balanced your dopamine, oxytocin, and serotonin collapse.
Your brain keeps scanning for their signal, desperate to restore regulation.
You check your phone, scroll their page, replay memories — all attempts to keep the loop alive.

You're not weak; you're wired.
Love isn't just emotional — it's neurological.
Heartbreak is the body detoxing from attachment.

The silence hurts most because the loop can't close.
The mind wants resolution, the body wants safety, and neither can find it.
So you spin.

Rumination isn't obsession — it's your brain trying to fix a broken pattern with no input left to process.

The Spiral — Rumination Loop

You replay every word, every glance.
What did I do wrong?
Could I have fixed it?

Why wasn't I enough?

That isn't weakness — it's programming.
Your mind is a pattern-recognition machine trying to solve an emotional equation that no longer computes.

It's painful, but it's sacred.
This is where you finally meet yourself — where your pain becomes your teacher.

The Recovery — Rebuilding New Loops

Healing isn't time passing.
It's repetition rewired.

Each day you choose a new path, you teach your brain that safety lives somewhere else now.
You breathe instead of text.
You write instead of spiral.
You walk instead of wait.

The flood of grief becomes a river.
The river becomes a stream.
The stream becomes a trickle.

That's not forgetting — that's your nervous system rewriting the code.

You stop waiting for closure and start creating peace.
You realize that love didn't leave you — it transformed.
It became self-respect, awareness, and boundaries.

Patterns Over Promises

People tell you who they are through repetition, not apology.
Stop believing words. Watch behavior.

If someone says they'll change but the loop stays the same — believe the loop.
If love feels like anxiety instead of calm, trust your body, not their story.

Red flags are intuition in motion. Trust it. It won't steer you wrong.

Patterns are data.
And data never lies.

The Rebuild — The Love That Lasts

Love doesn't heal you.
Awareness does.

Once you see your loops clearly, you stop chasing chaos and start choosing peace.
You stop trying to "fix" people who mistake your empathy for fuel.
You stop calling intensity connection.

Healing isn't the absence of love — it's the birth of healthy love.

A healthy relationship doesn't feel like adrenaline; it feels like exhale.
It's calm, not boring.
It's trust, not tension.
It's communication without punishment, honesty without fear, space without disconnection.

In healthy love, two people regulate each other without losing themselves.
There's laughter that feels easy, silence that feels safe, and conflict that becomes collaboration.
You don't have to beg to be seen — you're already understood.

That's what awareness creates: two people who can name their loops and choose to grow instead of repeat.
They mirror healing, not wounds.
They build, not drain.

One night, while traveling, I sat beside an older couple celebrating forty-five years of marriage.
I asked, "What's the secret?"
The husband smiled and said, "We never stopped evolving together."

That's it. That's the loop that lasts.
Not perfection. Not fantasy.

Evolution — two people consciously choosing to keep expanding toward one another.

The best relationships aren't found; they're built.
Brick by brick. Breath by breath.
Through awareness, communication, and the courage to repair.

That's love.
Not a destination — a direction.
Not a fairy tale — a feedback loop of growth.

That's the love that spirals upward — the kind that outlives the storm.

Closing — The Heart's True Work

Love isn't meant to complete you.
It's meant to mirror you — to show what still needs healing.

When two people regulate, repair, and rise together, they become medicine — not just for each other, but for everyone who feels their peace.

That's the love worth waiting for.
Not the one that burns bright and fades,
but the one that burns steady and transforms.

Because in the end, love isn't who you fall for.
It's who you rise with.

CHAPTER 13

The Illusion of Fear

Fear isn't the monster hiding in the dark.
It's the shadow cast by the things we refuse to let go of.

We spend our lives thinking we're running from fear itself —
but really, we're running from meaning.
From the weight we've attached to losing, failing, changing, or being seen.

It's not the fall that terrifies us.
It's what we've convinced ourselves the fall will say about who we are.

Fear of Failure

You're not afraid of failure.
You're afraid of what you've made failure mean about you.

Because somewhere along the way, you tied your worth to winning.
You mistook perfection for proof of value.
And every stumble feels like a mirror reflecting the parts of you you've yet to love.

But failure isn't your enemy — it's your teacher.
It's the quiet whisper saying, "There's still more of you to discover."

Fear of Being Alone

You're not afraid of being alone.
You're afraid of meeting yourself without distraction.

The silence isn't empty — it's honest.

It shows you where your company ends and your truth begins.
Most people call it loneliness, but it's just the echo of your own voice asking to be heard.

Sit with it long enough, and you realize —
solitude was never the absence of love,
it was the doorway back to it.

Fear of the Future

You're not afraid of the future.
You're afraid of losing control over the story you've already written.

You want life to stay inside the lines you drew before you knew who you were.
But the future isn't chaos — it's creation.
It's the universe giving you a blank page and asking, "Who are you now?"

Control isn't safety.
It's just resistance in disguise.

Fear of Rejection

You're not afraid of rejection.
You're afraid someone's "no" will confirm your own self-doubt.

It's not their silence that hurts —
it's the echo of all the times you silenced yourself.

But rejection isn't a closed door.
It's redirection — a mirror showing you where your energy no longer belongs.
Sometimes the universe removes people from your path
because they were never meant to walk beside your becoming.

Fear of Success

You're not afraid of success.
You're afraid of proving you were capable all along.

Because once you do, there's no one left to blame for the smallness you stayed in.
Success demands exposure — it reveals the part of you that can no longer hide behind potential.

It's not the spotlight that burns —
it's the truth that you were always worthy of standing in it.

Fear of Change

You're not afraid of change.
You're afraid that the version of you built on survival won't survive it.

Every ending feels like death to the ego,
but endings are how the soul breathes.
Transformation doesn't destroy you — it edits you.
And sometimes, the only way to become who you're meant to be
is to stop being who you were taught to be.

Fear of Love

You're not afraid of love.
You're afraid of being truly seen.

Because when love finds you, it strips you of your armor.
It asks you to be naked in ways that have nothing to do with skin.
Love isn't always comfortable —
it's truth dressed in vulnerability.

And once you've been seen,
you can't pretend to be invisible again.

Fear of Death

You're not afraid of dying.
You're afraid of never having truly lived.

Because deep down, you know the body ends,
but the story doesn't.
And the tragedy isn't in death —
it's in reaching it without ever becoming fully alive.

Death isn't the full stop —
it's the ellipsis between chapters.
A reminder that life was always meant to loop.

The Truth Beneath It All

Every fear is a loop.
An orbit around something you've yet to face.
When you finally turn toward it,
you realize it was never darkness chasing you —
it was light waiting to be seen.

On the other side of fear isn't safety.
It's freedom.

And that's the point of it all —
to stop running from the shadow,
and remember that you were the light, the whole

CHAPTER 14

Rewiring the Loop

When Anxiety Takes Over

Anxiety used to run my life.
There were nights I'd lie in bed replaying images of my ex with someone else. My heart would race, my chest would tighten, and the same scene would loop like a movie I couldn't turn off. It wasn't the images that were killing me — it was the meaning I attached to them.

One night, I hit a breaking point. My breath was short, my mind was screaming, and I felt trapped in my own body. Then I remembered the 3-6-9 breath:

Inhale for 3.
Hold for 6.
Exhale for 9.

With every exhale, I whispered, "That ain't my circus. I choose peace. I move forward."
At first it felt pointless — but after a few rounds, the storm eased. The thoughts didn't vanish, but I wasn't their prisoner anymore. I realized I didn't have to stop the loop — I just had to step out of it.

When Addiction Calls

There was a point in my life when I couldn't go a single day without a drink. What started as weekend fun became dependency. Crown Royal was my comfort, my escape, my routine. Little by little, it consumed me until the bottle felt like my only friend.

When I finally put it down, I didn't know what to do with the hours I used to spend drinking. That's when I realized recovery isn't about erasing yesterday's destructive loops — it's about choosing new constructive ones today.

Alcohol, food, sex — they're everywhere. You can't hide from them.
But you can replace them.

I filled the space with what made me feel alive instead of numb: hiking, mountain biking, spending time with my daughter, painting, reading. We were cutting a new path through the grass and letting the old trail grow over. The cravings still come in waves, but the more you live through constructive loops, the quieter they get.

When You Feel Numb

There are days when you can't get off the couch.
Not because you're lazy, but because your body is carrying decades of destructive loops — stored pain, fear, and shame clogging your system.

The antidote is movement.
You don't need a gym. Move however you can — stretch, dance, walk, breathe.
Each step tells your nervous system, "I'm still here. I'm still moving."
Flow is medicine.

When You Need a Break from Life — Step Into the Forest

Nature became my therapy.
There was a calm I felt the moment I stepped into the forest that I never found anywhere else. It was as if the trees absorbed my noise — the chaos in my head, the tension in my chest — and handed it back as stillness.

In Japan, they call it Shinrin-yoku — forest bathing.
It's not hiking. It's not exercise. It's immersion. You walk slowly, breathe deeply, and let nature re-tune your nervous system.

Science backs what the soul already knows: trees release compounds that help reduce stress; beneath your feet, the mycorrhizal web connects roots for miles — a living internet of life, sharing nutrients and information.

That's what healing looks like: connection, reciprocity, presence.
I stopped searching for peace and started feeling it — the wind through the leaves, rivers rapids playing a song, the warmth of sunshine on my skin.

When the Past Returns — Meet the Shadow

Carl Jung called it the Shadow — the basement of the soul. Everything you hide ends up running your life from the dark.

My Shadow showed up as anger, control, and shame.
When I stopped fighting it and started listening, I realized each emotion was trying to protect me. That's when I met him — the little boy version of me.

I pictured little Paul: scared, feeling unloved, unworthy. I sat with him. I told him he's special. That he doesn't have to be scared anymore. That he's loved, and he's going to be okay. Something in me softened. The anger loosened. The shame lost its grip. When you love the child inside you, the adult finally heals too.
If you can, find a therapist. They're not there to fix you — they're there to help you turn on the light. Healing isn't weakness; it's intelligence.

When You Need Clarity — Pick Up the Pen

Journaling has been my lifeline.
We all carry things we think we could never say out loud — but paper listens.

I never got to say goodbye to my dad before he died. I carried that guilt for years until I wrote him a letter, telling him everything I wished I'd said.
I can't change that he's gone, but I can change the weight I carry.

Whatever you're feeling, write it down.
Fears shrink on paper. Goals become tangible. This is where you get to talk to you.
No right or wrong — just truth finding its way out.

When You Need Perspective — Gratitude

Anytime I was going through something heavy, my mom would say, "Write a gratitude list." It sounded too simple — until I did it.

Gratitude shifts your focus from what's missing to what's already here. It reminds your mind you're not in danger — you're alive, supported, surrounded by small miracles you forgot to notice.

You don't have to write a novel — just three things, every day.
Clean water. Your child's laughter. The sunrise.
Write them. Feel them. Let them sink in.

Gratitude is the fastest way out of autopilot and back into presence.
And presence is where peace lives.

When Your Mind Spins — Use Mantras

When your mind won't stop racing, it isn't broken — it's trying to close open loops. That's why you replay arguments, imagine outcomes, and invent stories that keep you stuck. Your brain wants completion.

Mantras became my mental anchor — new code that told my brain, We're done running that program.

When I felt the urge to reach out to my ex, I'd stop, breathe, and say: "I am unshakable. I choose calm. I move forward."

At first it felt forced. Then it started to work. Each repetition signaled: you don't have to seek the familiar anymore — not her, not the bottle, not the chaos. Those loops aren't home; peace is.

Mantras are messages from your higher self to your survival self.
Repeat them until they become truth — and then live like they already are.

When You Can't Calm Down — Train the Nervous System

I'd lived in fight-or-flight for years — stepdad rage, running from cops, running from heartbreak. My mind and body were addicted to survival. I had to teach them I was safe again.

The cold plunge became my classroom.
As I lowered into freezing water, every instinct screamed, Get out.
But I stayed. Hand over heart, I whispered, "I'm safe. I'm not in danger. This is discomfort. I'm in control."
If I can push past the resistance of cold water, I can push past the resistance of life. The body learns through experience, not words. Each time you make peace with discomfort, your nervous system rewires for strength.

Closing Reflection — Coming Home

Every tool in this chapter — breath, movement, journaling, gratitude, mantra, stillness, cold, nature — is a way to bring you back home to yourself.
Not to fix what's broken, but to remember you were never broken. You were running old loops.

Coming home isn't a place.
It's a feeling — the moment your soul exhales and says, "I'm safe now."
When your mind quiets, your body softens, and your heart finally believes what's always been true:

You matter.

CHAPTER 15

Fate & Collision

Fate isn't mystery.
It's motion.
It's the quiet geometry of energy folding into itself, again and again, until two paths finally meet.

People call it chance when they collide with love, heartbreak, or awakening.
But nothing about the universe is random.
Every thought, every choice, every vibration you send into the field moves outward like a ripple.
And ripples meet.

That meeting—the collision—is fate.
Not destiny written in the stars, but mathematics unfolding in real time.
The equation of energy searching for equilibrium.

◻

Two people crossing in a grocery aisle might just be filling their carts,
but beneath that moment are years of decisions, heartbreaks, detours, and delays,
all spiraling into a single point in time.

Every missed turn led them there.
Every "wrong" relationship, every job that fell apart, every night they thought they'd failed—
was the choreography of collision.
Not punishment. Not luck.
Precision.

You don't meet people by accident.
You meet them because your frequencies matched long enough for the universe to say now.

When two loops overlap, they create interference patterns—just like sound waves.
Sometimes they harmonize. Sometimes they distort.
That's why one person brings peace and another brings chaos.
You aren't being tested; you're being tuned.

Carl Jung said, "Until you make the unconscious conscious, it will direct your life and you will call it fate."
Fate isn't written for you—it's written by you, in the language of your loops.
Every thought you repeat is a brushstroke on the canvas of reality.
Every emotion you feed shapes the frequency of what comes next.

The liar finds mirrors of deception.
The wounded attract the wounded.
The aware meet the awake.

It's not superstition—it's resonance.
You don't get what you want.
You get what you are.

When frequencies clash, you feel it—
the heat, the static, the friction.
You call it drama, heartbreak, bad timing.
But what you're really feeling is the universe correcting your orbit.
Two energies trying to occupy the same space without alignment.

And when they harmonize?
You feel flow.
The coincidence that makes too much sense.
The stranger who speaks the truth you were just thinking.
The song that plays the moment you need it most.

That's not randomness.
That's rhythm.
The universe winking back.

Life moves like a great river—
you are both the current and the driftwood,
the cause and the consequence.

Every collision redirects your flow.
The heartbreak that forced you to grow.
The failure that rerouted your purpose.

The detour that revealed your destiny.

The universe isn't punishing you; it's aligning you.
Every disruption is a re-calibration.
Every ending is a beginning disguised as correction.

Tesla saw it in vibration.
Jung saw it in psyche.
Watts felt it in the breath between moments.

They all spoke of the same law—
that energy seeks harmony,
and consciousness is the conductor.

So when life collapses, don't fight the fall.
Fall consciously.
Trust that gravity has its own grace.
What leaves your orbit was never meant to stay.
What returns, returns renewed.
Fate is not the hand of a god.
It's the echo of your own energy returning home.

The question isn't whether the universe is listening—
it's whether you are.

Because once you start listening,
you stop chasing.
You stop forcing.
You begin to see—
that everything and everyone crossing your path
is part of the same great conversation of cause and effect,
looping endlessly,
perfectly,
back to you.

CHAPTER 16

Loops in Others

When awareness cracks open, the world stops feeling random.
You start to notice the rhythm under everything—
the way people talk, flinch, smile, avoid, defend.
Every moment between humans is a loop unfolding in real time.

No one is broken.
They're just running the code they learned to survive.

You see it in the friend who always keeps things light because depth once hurt him.
In the woman who never lets anyone help because needing once felt like weakness.
In the guy at the bar talking too loud because silence feels like rejection.
Each of them repeating the emotion they never resolved.

We call it personality, but most of it is protection.

Walk into a room and you'll feel it before you understand it.
The couple smiling too wide after a fight.
The coworker whose laughter feels like armor.
The stranger whose tension fills the air before a word is spoken.
You don't need language for this—your body reads theirs.
That pull in your chest? That's resonance.
You're tuning to their frequency.

It's the same reason you leave some conversations drained and others peaceful.
We're transmitters. Constantly.
Trading signals, borrowing moods, syncing nervous systems without a word.

Once you see that, judgment fades.
The angry man isn't your enemy—he's still fighting ghosts.
The cold one isn't heartless—she's protecting something fragile.
The liar isn't evil—he's terrified of being small.

Everyone you meet is trying to finish a story they didn't start.
And when you understand that, compassion replaces reaction.

You stop matching energy; you start mastering it.
You stop asking, "Why are they doing this to me?"
and start wondering, "What loop in them—and in me—is playing out right now?"

You'll see loops everywhere:
the couple that breaks up and gets back together like clockwork,
the friend who's always "too busy" for peace,
the coworker who thrives on crisis because calm feels foreign.
They aren't choosing misery—they're following the path carved deepest in their mind.
Water follows the groove it knows. So do we.

Until one day, someone—maybe you—decides to change the flow.

Awareness doesn't shout.
It pauses.
It becomes the still point in a spinning room.
It's the deep breath that breaks generations of reflex.

You can't fix anyone's loop.
You can only become still enough that yours doesn't feed theirs.
Presence is gravity—it settles chaos by example.
When you're grounded, people feel it.
They exhale without knowing why.

That's how healing moves through the world: quietly.
Not through preaching, but through peace that hums louder than noise.

Tesla would've called it coherence.
Jung would've called it integration.
Watts would've smiled and said, "Now you're dancing with the current."

When two people meet in awareness, they stop colliding—they start orbiting.
Conversation flows.
Silence feels safe.
Connection becomes creation.

And when friction returns, you no longer see it as conflict.
You see it as feedback.

The universe fine-tuning harmony.

That's the moment you become untouchable—not cold, not distant, but steady.
You can stand in someone else's storm and still see the stars.

That's awareness.
That's love without condition.
The loop made conscious.

CHAPTER 17

The Loop of Legacy

When you heal a loop, it doesn't end with you.
It ripples outward — through family, through strangers, through time.
You become the correction in a lineage that never had the words for its own wounds.

We inherit more than features.
We inherit fear, silence, sacrifice, addiction, pride.
Every family passes something down — some pass opportunity,
but most pass survival.
Generations stitched together not by wealth,
but by grit.

Your father learned to shut down because no one ever listened.
Your mother learned to over-give because love once came with conditions.
Your grandparents carried secrets like stones in their pockets — too heavy to name, too sacred to drop.
And now you stand here, holding all of it, wondering why your chest feels full of stories that aren't even yours.

That ache in your gut isn't weakness.
It's inheritance asking to be rewritten.

You are not the curse.
You are the chance it finally breaks.

Science calls it epigenetics —
trauma leaving fingerprints on DNA, memory etched into biology.
But our ancestors didn't need the term.
They already knew pain could echo through blood.
They prayed so their children might sleep lighter.
They built so someone, someday, could rest.

Every loop that harmed them was an unfinished equation.

You're here to balance it.

Healing doesn't always look like light and incense.
Sometimes it looks like choosing silence instead of shouting.
Sometimes it's holding your child a little longer than your parents held you.
Sometimes it's letting someone love you without earning it first.

That's how the chain breaks — not in grand gestures,
but in micro-decisions that rewrite centuries.
The way you speak becomes a new language.
The way you listen becomes an inheritance.

One calm father rewires a generation.
One honest mother changes the chemistry of a family tree.
One I forgive you alters the orbit of an entire bloodline.

Forgiveness doesn't erase the past; it reroutes it.
You begin to see your parents not as heroes or villains, but as echoes —
voices repeating the only song they were taught.
They weren't cruel; they were conditioned.
They weren't absent; they were afraid.
And maybe, for the first time, you can look back with understanding instead of blame.

That's redemption — the quiet kind.
The kind that doesn't demand applause because it already feels eternal.

Every conscious act adds to the field.
The energy you hold today becomes someone else's baseline tomorrow.
Your peace becomes their starting point.
Your awareness becomes their map.

You are not just living your life; you are shaping what life means for those who come next.
Your choices are architecture.
Your love, a new law of physics written into the family code.

Legacy isn't about what you leave behind when you die.
It's what you transmit while you live.

And someday, when someone you love faces their own storm,

they'll pause before reacting —
and they won't know why.
They'll just feel it: the echo of your stillness.
The calm you built into the bloodstream.

They'll find peace faster because you found it first.
They'll breathe deeper because you decided to stop holding your breath.
They'll love better because you showed them it was safe to.

That's legacy.
Not the name. Not the fortune.
The frequency.

If your ancestors could see you now,
they'd recognize that look in your eyes —
the same fire they carried when the world felt impossible.
Only now it burns for freedom instead of survival.

And if your children could speak to you decades from now,
they'd thank you — not for being perfect,
but for being aware.
For facing the darkness without passing it forward.

Because awareness is love in motion.
It's what turns pain into wisdom, and blood into blessing.

You are the hinge between what was and what will be.
The bridge between survival and creation.
The living proof that loops don't just repeat —
they can evolve.

And as the wheel turns,
you'll feel it —
that quiet pulse beneath everything,
the rhythm of those who came before you
and those who'll come after,
all moving through the same breath,
the same loop,
made lighter because you dared to change it.

This is the climb.
The storm is behind you, the summit ahead.
You've seen the loops. You've lived them. You've learned their language.

Now you stand in their center —
not a prisoner,
but the one who turned pain into pattern,
pattern into purpose,
and purpose into peace.

CHAPTER 18

The Cosmic Loop

A heartbeat.
A breath.
Air in, air out — the oldest rhythm you'll ever know.
It's been happening since before you were born and it will go on long after your name is dust.

That's a loop — life moving through you.

Every system inside you runs on rhythm.
Your heart beats in patterns.
Your lungs move like tides.
Your neurons fire like lightning returning to the same clouds.
You are a living pattern pretending to be a person.

Step outside and the pattern continues.
The wind hums in waves.
Oceans inhale and exhale against the shore.
Cities breathe — morning rush, evening rest, the same pulse in concrete form.
From galaxies spiraling outward to atoms dancing in silence, everything repeats itself into existence.

Nothing in the universe travels in a straight line.
Everything curves back home.

Nature remembers what we forget.
The trees shed what no longer serves them and wait, patient, for spring.
The stars never doubt their brightness.
The sun doesn't apologize for rising again.
Only humans fight the rhythm — clutching at control, mistaking predictability for safety.

But the universe has never been late.
And neither have you.

You think you missed your chance — you didn't.
You think you took the wrong turn — you didn't.
You are exactly where the current needs you to be — a small loop in a vast design still unfolding.

Tesla said, "If you want to find the secrets of the universe, think in terms of energy, frequency, and vibration."
He wasn't speaking in metaphors; he was describing the operating system of reality.

Everything vibrates.
Every thought, every emotion, every cell in your body hums at a frequency.
Each one sends ripples into the field and receives them back.
You are both transmitter and receiver, forever tuning and being tuned.
You are exactly where the current needs you to be — a small loop in a vast design still unfolding.

It doesn't punish or reward.
It reflects.

Change the vibration within, and the universe rearranges to match it.
That's not mysticism.
That's resonance.

You've felt it before.
Thinking of someone right before they call.
Hearing the perfect lyric at the exact moment you needed it.
Meeting a stranger who says one sentence that changes everything.
That isn't coincidence — that's coherence.

When you're aligned, life stops resisting and starts responding.
The current carries you instead of crushing you.
Synchronicity becomes the language of the divine.

Even what you call bad luck has purpose.
The detours, heartbreaks, delays — they aren't blocks.
They're corrections.
Life doesn't break you; it bends you back into alignment.

When the forest burns, it fertilizes the soil.
When the wave collapses, it gathers strength for the next rise.
You're built the same way.

The universe refines itself through your resilience.

You are made of the same dust that built mountains,
the same fire that forged stars,
the same ocean that carves canyons.
You are the cosmos slowed down enough to feel itself.

So when life feels heavy, remember: it's not chaos — it's calibration.
You're not being punished; you're being tuned.
Every challenge is the universe striking the note you were meant to vibrate at.

You were never behind.
You were never separate.
You are the loop becoming aware of itself — a fragment of infinity learning how to love in form.

Take a breath.
Feel your pulse.
That's the same rhythm that turns galaxies.

You don't need to chase enlightenment; you are what it looks like when consciousness learns to breathe.
Every inhale writes a beginning.
Every exhale lets the story continue.

Keep moving.
Keep trusting the flow.
Keep choosing curiosity over control, love over fear.

Because the moment you surrender, the whole universe exhales with you.

You are the spark, the pattern, the pulse.
You are the cosmic loop — infinite, evolving, alive.

Shoot for the stars,
because you are one.

Final Chapter

The Upward Spiral

I've walked through hell to become the man I am.
Childhood trauma. Prison walls. Betrayal. Heartbreak. Failure.
Those things don't define me — they refined me.
They carved grooves deep enough for truth to flow through.

I see them now for what they were: lessons.
Opportunities to grow.
Invitations to turn pain into purpose.

If there's one thing this book leaves behind, it's this:
No matter what you've done or lost, you matter.
You were never a mistake.
The fact that you're still breathing means life isn't finished with you yet.

None of the things we chase truly matter — not the likes, cars, houses, or image.
What matters is living *intentionally*.
Feeling the heartbeat of life again.

Watch the sunrise while the world is quiet.
Smell the rain returning to earth.
Dance barefoot in your kitchen.
Sit on the floor and let your children climb into your lap.
Take the trip. Say yes.
Walk away from what no longer serves you — even when it hurts.
Reconnect with earth, breath, and belonging.

Because when the lights go out — when your final loop ends — none of the noise will matter.
You'll think about sunsets, laughter, and the moments you were *fully alive*.

That's real success:
Leaving the world softer than you found it.
Leaving people lighter than when they met you.

Building a legacy made of kindness and love.

Love is the meaning of life.
It always has been.
If everything you say, do, and think comes from love, there can be no wrong.
Love turns chaos into peace, darkness into light.
It saves us — every single time.

So if no one's told you lately:
You're not broken.
You do matter.
And I love you.
I'm proud of you.
Because choosing to heal — to live awake and from the heart — is the bravest thing a human can do.

Take this truth with you:
Every loop you've lived brought you here for a reason.
Every breath is a chance to begin again.
Every choice, an opportunity to spiral upward.

The goal was never perfection — it was evolution.
To turn pain into purpose.
Destruction into design.
To take the loop you were given and make it more beautiful for whoever comes next.

That's how the world changes — one awakened loop at a time.
One heart choosing love over fear.
One person deciding to live wide awake.

That's how we spiral upward.
That's how we heal the world.
That's how you remember — once and for all —

You were the pattern all along.

You Matter.
You Always Have.
And You Always Will.

Made in the USA
Coppell, TX
19 January 2026

67908366R00046